The Heart Remembers

HESHNA BHAGAWAN

The Heart Remembers
Copyright © 2025 by Heshna Bhagawan.

MILTON & HUGO L.L.C.
4407 Park Ave., Suite 5
Union City, NJ 07087, USA

Website: *www. miltonandhugo.com*
Hotline: *1- 888-778-0033*
Email: *info@miltonandhugo.com*

Ordering Information:
Quantity sales. Special discounts are granted to corporations, associations, and other organizations. For more information on these discounts, please reach out to the publisher using the contact information provided above.

Library of Congress Control Number: 2025910966
ISBN-13:   979-8-89285-556-3   [Paperback Edition]
                979-8-89285-587-7   [Hardback Edition]
                979-8-89285-555-6   [Digital Edition]

Rev. date: 06/18/2025

Dedication

To my past selves,

I know you thought you would never find the surface
again. Somewhere beneath it all, there was a light. This
book is for the part of you that remembers how to shine,
even when you're deep underwater. The healing journey
is an endless path. Healing is not your purpose. Nobody
is coming to save you, you save yourself. Thank you for
doing everything you could to survive. I am grateful for
everything you have done.

Now it is time to live. Simply focus on your living while
taking care of yourself and those around you. Once you
find peace, guard it fiercely. Let go of anyone who brings
chaos upon your calm and find wisdom in the chaos. Stay
open to abundance, whether it be money, love, or peace.
Continue to keep your arms open. Life will rise and fall.
Accept it all and just live. Be present. Practice gratitude.

With love,
Always

Pretty Hurts

When you were little, some phrases that never made
sense,
warnings and whispers that would someday weigh
on you.
Ice-cold hands froze your body, each touch a chill that
crept deeper,
winter's breath wrapping around your bones.
Confused, you unconsciously allowed the negative
energy to consume you.
When you realized you were trapped beneath the
unauthentic chains,
You opened your heart for love, which was enough to
break the chains.
I am proud of you for keeping your boundaries intact
while becoming gentle.

Destined to be a lover girl but forced to watch them make you temporarily feel like the only girl in the world.

Your intuition screams at you that they don't care. Instead of trusting it, you believe your delusional side while making excuses to keep them around.

They say fools fall in love fast, is it wrong to believe in love?

Even if it's fleeting, even if it burns bright and fades rapidly like fireworks.

Is it wrong to believe that your soulmate is out there?

Despite them leaving you once the testosterone runs out, and you were just a pretty girl to them.

Continue to be a fool who believes in love.

Like the trees let go of their leaves during autumn and endure the coldness of the harsh chills.

Outside for months, stripped of color for months, enduring the winter's weight.

In spring, the leaves return, tender green against the last frost, and in summer they bloom and radiate their energy to all living beings.

That is how you will rise again, forgiving yourself anew each season.

Why should you give up on love for those who didn't know how to love you?

Your time will come and you will be loved the way you love others.

All you yearned for is genuine energy.

Whether it be friends, colleagues, or lovers.

The consistent shunning or hazing shut you off completely.

You built walls around your heart, a fortress against rejection.

Each crack in that wall is made by those patient enough to care,

letting love seep in, softening the stone with each touch.

Love always wins and you allow others to love you.

Solitude is the cost, it seems, of staying true to yourself, especially in a world that reduced you to appearances. No matter how hard you worked or how much you studied, they were always so quick to point out your flaws.

Sometimes, they even make you feel guilty for your accomplishments,
By hitting you with reality checks that diminishes your success.
Most women want to be your friends for the sake of competition.
Whilst most men just want a chance to see if they can lay with you.
Let's not forget the catcalling that gets even more cringe as you get older.
After getting catcalled in an outfit, you feel disgust everytime you see that outfit.
So you constantly tell yourself, "It is my body and I won't let a man's opinion change me."
You were afraid to let your guards down.
Like a wild animal, you adopted the flight or fight response anytime someone got too close.
Flight has always been your first choice.

Whenever someone gets close to seeing your scars, you feel as if they would drown in your ocean of suffering and flee.

Instead, the right people will stay and accept you.

They will support you while you direct your ocean to the seeds meant for you, so you can grow.

Thank you for holding on to those who actually respect you instead of pushing them away.

You refused to let people's opinions change who you are due to understanding that your validation is all you need.

It is a lonely journey because of the amount of time people are always leaving you.

Sometimes, your family were too busy with their own lives to even be there for you.

Despite giving you everything they could, your quest continues.

Not because your family lacked, you want to learn who you are beyond gifts.

Besides, it is your family's first time living, just like it is yours.

You love your family with all your heart.

At times, the journey felt so lonely that you imagined what your life would've been like if you looked different.

You endured so much pain that you attempted to make yourself less appealing.

Of course it translated as you letting go of yourself and making yourself look "ugly."

It truly made you wonder: "Is beauty a curse?"

On some days, beauty felt like armor—a shield from vulnerability.

But other times, it felt like glass, fragile and distorting,
reflecting others' their insecurities back at them.
I am so thankful that you are now embracing who
you are.
I am proud of you for learning how to love yourself and
enjoy your own company.

True beauty comes from within.
Embrace your reflection, its scars, its beauty, its
strength
like a fire that never dims.
Be that adult for yourself, now and forever,
a flame that never dims, a strength that never fades.

Forgotten Memories

When you are young, everything is a mystery.

You are unaware of the rights and wrongs.

But our bodies senses when anything doesn't feel right.

So it locks the memories in a chest.

To unlock the chest, we must reach a certain level of maturity.

Once we reach that level of maturity, it bursts open without any warnings.

It drives us insane.

Some people shoves those memories down because they believe their feelings are not valid,

so they seek out temporary distractions to forget the memories.

Whereas other people sit in their pain and allow themselves to feel and let it go,

When it hurts too much, they seek help.

You are worthy of healing and your feelings are valid.

Thank you for choosing yourself and saving yourself.

Growing up too fast

The catcalling started when you were too young to
even know the meaning.
Eight year old you thought it was bullying.
As you grew older, whenever a man complimented you,
you felt oversexualized.
So you stay away from the opposite gender.

Yet you crave for that emotional intimate connection.
Of course, you are secure in yourself.
But a part of you wonders what it is like to have
someone who loves the same way you do.
Post depression hits you and now you are living like a
sixty year old, in a twenty-year old's body.
You sit and wonder what your life would've been like if
you had the same chance other people your age had.

What would life have been like if you hadn't been on
survival mode for so long?

You grew up fast but there is nothing you can do.
It made you humble and feel more empathy for others.
You no longer judge others because everyone has a story.
The right people stand by your side and
understand you.
You haven't missed out on anything.

Your blessings were meant to be huge.
You are not boring because you can relate to an eighty
year old.
It means, you had to mentally grow to accept the divine
blessings coming your way.
The lessons are there for you to love yourself more.
The journey forced you to stay strong because you are
your own saviour.
Nobody is coming to save you.

You stayed strong and learned to accept compliments.
Thank you for being so strong and always choosing love
no matter what.

Forgiving myself

Forgiving yourself is a never ending journey.

We are all human beings who are always growing and healing.

Certain situations are repeated to see if you have truly forgiven yourself.

Sometimes life becomes harsh, when the storm creeps in, life throws in tornados, hurricanes, earthquakes, or tsunamis.

Then you get stuck in a hole.

As you are trying to escape, you grasp a hold of the perfect part that will lunge your body out of the hole.

Just as you lunge upwards, life pushes you deeper into the hole.

Then just as you get close to the top again, life pushes you down even further.

Your body aches, yearning for a way out.

You become desperate and you want to see the light again.

But you choose to rest for a bit, waiting for your body to heal.

Life pushed you deep enough, now it is time to see the light.

Just as you attempt to escape, life pushes you even deeper into the hole.

Your body aches a hundred times more.

The fatigue rapidly consumes your body.

You lay there frozen, in pain.

Nobody can hear your screams.

You reflect and you wait for your body to heal again.

Once you are ready, you see a pole descending into the hole.

Someone heard you.

You begin climbing and just as you get close to the top, darkness creeps in.

Lightning strikes and there you go again falling.

As you hit the bottom, life pushes you down even more.

This time you are drowning in muddy water.

The rain is pouring hard.

Your chest feels frozen as you attempt to move around the thick liquid of sorrow.

The fight doesn't stop because you believe that one day you will see the light.

The pole disappeared and you are left there alone.

When your body gives up the fight, the water begins to drain into the hole.

The ground is dry but you are left in the puddle of agony.

There you are laying and resting, allowing your body to heal before you attempt to escape.

You stare into the sky and feel your body healing.

In the mist of chaos, you still feel grateful for the cells recreating themselves.

The palm of your hand is gently placed on your heart.
You feel that miraculous heartbeat and you feel your
skin fold when the smile wrinkles appear. Instead of
worrying how you will get to the light, you practice
gratitude for the things you currently have.
We are all worthy of abundance.
We must forgive ourselves fully for that one belief we
once ought to be true about ourselves.

Forgiving myself part 2

You always wondered what the meaning of
forgiveness is.
Was it forgiving that version of yourself for believing it
was the right thing to do?
You handled that so well.
Sitting in with your pool of agony, you realized that
their actions didn't hurt you as much.
It was the scenario you created that never manifested
into reality,
The scenario where they never hurt you.
Perhaps in a parallel universe, they never hurt you.
Instead of anger, sympathy fills your heart for those
who hurt you,
After all, hurt people hurt people.
Thank you for never allowing the bitter people to turn
you bitter.

You allowed yourself to sit in your pain by going back to those memories.

Then you visited that younger version that sabotaged your success,

The one who was too hurt to feel the pain so they repressed the emotions.

You embrace that younger version of yourself because they were just trying to protect you.

Grieving for the person you could've become had your past been different,

You created a eulogy to bid farewell to the hurt version of you.

Then you thank them for holding on and reassure them that they are safe.

After spending many years shaming yourself, you realized it was not your fault.

It was life teaching you lessons to built your character.

I am proud you have forgiven yourself to the extent that you no longer feel embarrassed for your past. Choosing to live instead of surviving is the most loving action you have chosen for yourself.

Surrendering

Here you are on your knees because you've
surrendered.
The numbness creeps into your body.
The weight of the suffering begins to take a toll.
Your attempt to stand up fails so you throw your
hands up.
Every ache in your body was a poignant reminder.
"Gosh you are so strong" - everyone keeps telling you the
same thing.
You are tired of being strong.
Instead of resting to prepare yourself to survive
another battle,
You are resting to prepare yourself to live life.
Living for the small moments.
Sunlight kissing and caressing your skin,
Making your skin glow like gold and honey combined.
Watching the sunrise and sunsets with your loved ones.
Chasing the stars and other astronomical events.

Preparing the most delicious and appealing meals to nourish your beautiful body.

Exercising because you love your health.

Using the time to stop and appreciate your loved ones,

Even if it means spending time with them for just ten seconds.

Living means making time to be present.

Doing things because it brings you peace and nothing else.

Money is absent and you expect nothing in return.

To live is to genuinely care.

Despite the chaos, you turn on some music so you can shake off the despair.

As you slowly practice gratitude, you feel the agony leaving your body.

Now you are laying in a puddle of peace and light.

Everywhere you go, you are surrounded by love,

Whether it be couples, mother and daughters, sons and mothers, father and sons, father and daughters, friends, cousins, pets and their paw-rents.

Love is everywhere and with that comes kindness.

You begin to experience so much kindness,
Even the angry people feel your light and adjust their mood to show kindness towards you.
The aura shines even brighter and it elevates you out of the hole.
You are unaware of the elevation until you sit down and ponder.
One day, you chose to stop and ponder.
Time stops and here you are, taking in a deep breath,
Inhaling the soft air around you,
Feeling the materials around you,
Observing every movement around you.
Placing your hand on your heart and smiling,
"Thank you for keeping me alive"
A tsunami of gratitude rushes into your body.
The gratitude feeling emerges and that is when you feel your feet touch the ground,
because you have made it out of the dark hole.

Last 6 months

"You will be fine!"
You wish those words were magical spells, just like
Cinderella's godmother.
Like the godmother turned the mice into horses,
You wished those words made your heart whole again.
You smile and nod.
What else can you do?

Born with a hole in your heart,
You wonder, what void am I missing.
When you step outside, you lose yourself while staring
at others.
You stare at the families, wondering if you will have
your own someday.
When people compliment you, you know you may not
be here for a long time so you let them go.
You stare at the other people your age who are living
their life and wonder if you will ever get your turn.
Sometimes you wonder what life would've been like if
you could do it all over again, without the void.
What would life have been like if your life was all about
rainbows and butterflies?

Then you remember that with agony comes wisdom.
Wisdom is a shield of strength that keeps you on your
path to your goals.
So, you live everyday like it is your last.

Deep down inside, you are petrified.

What if this is it?

You want to live longer.

There are many sunsets to watch, whether it be alone or with company.

Grow old with a partner after you build an empire together.

Love so deep that your only fear is losing them.

Squeeze everything you want to do in case you never make it.

The surgeon said you must be 100% positive.

Just pretend.

So you have to be strong.

You had to pretend like you had your whole life ahead of you.

You do it for those who love you.

You came out a different person,

A grateful person that chose to live.

Accept where you are right now

Everything happens for a reason,
Whether it be for the best or the worst.
You are not behind, you are right on time.
You are not ahead, you are right on time.
Stop comparing your journey with others.
If you think you are ahead of everyone else, that is your
ego speaking.
If you think you are behind everyone around you, it is
coming from a place of lack.
Practice gratitude because you once prayed for the
moment you are in.
Even the darkest moment teaches you a lesson.
Sometimes life has to get rid of certain things so that
you can welcome better things with open arms, ready
to embrace it all.
If you lost someone, perhaps it is teaching you to
cherish those who are still around you.

Stop dwelling on the past and don't live in the future.
Be present.
Look around you, observe your environment. Take in
the scenery.
One day, during your best moments, you will get
triggered to go down a memory lane,
Whether it was a positive or negative memory, it will
teach you to be grateful.
Love, pray, practice gratitude, exercise, meditate,
and eat.
Do whatever it takes for you to appreciate the present
moment.

The Woman that Needs No Man

Deep down inside, you believe in true love.
But you haven't met your man yet,
and the ones you met made you lose hope.
Every rejection represented a brick in the wall you built
to protect yourself.
The cement that sealed the walls together was your
comfort in solitude.
It was only you, and you were afraid to be seen.
Every battle fought alone formed an ice shield.
It was a never ending winter box sealed with darkness.

One day, while grieving a lost one, a light came and told
you to "open your heart to love".
It melted the ice away and stripped the bricked walls
down.
As the doubts built the walls again, the universe began
sending love your way.
It was everywhere.

Even after seeing your scars, they stayed.
Love makes you feel validated, especially self-love.
You trusted yourself so much that you always chose
yourself.
I am grateful for you and the way you handled
everything you endured alone.
Thank you for being patient and always choosing love.

When it felt pointless for a man to come into your life
because solitude became your best friend.
Love bid farewell to the belief that "nobody will ever
love me."

The person that you are meant to be with proved it all
wrong.

If you don't believe in love, how will it find you?
What if there is someone out there who can provide
the love and safe space you deserve?
You are your savior.
Become your own dream woman
while patiently waiting for your soulmate.
Make your inner child proud
by becoming the woman she looked up to.
Your soulmate is out there if you believe they exist.
A man who knows you can do it all alone,
But insists on being there because he wants to be there
for you.
He does it all out of love because you are the woman he
prayed and wished for!
Just like you prayed and wished for him.
You are everything he ever wanted in his wife, you are
his dream woman.
He is everything you ever wanted in your husband, he
is your dream man.

Weird Girl

Comparison is the thief of joy,
But you can't help watching others who were fortunate
enough to develop their social interaction skills.
You were busy surviving.
You stare at those your age and you wonder, what if I
was normal.
That mindset came from a place of lack and I am
grateful you recognize it.

Sometimes people make fun of you for being different, for being weird.

They assumed you were slow but in reality, your mind couldn't relax.

Stuck in survival mode, you couldn't focus well enough.

They ridicule you for being too quiet.

They thought you didn't know what they were doing and so they made fun of you.

You stopped talking to people because it became difficult to differentiate the genuine from the fake ones.

Into the world of solitude and you escaped with distractions, addictions.

You chose books and video games.

You knew. You knew that they made fun of you for being slow sometimes.

You knew they only wanted to talk to you so they could ridicule you even more.

You knew that they thought you were childish, too clueless to comprehend their jokes.

With books, you escaped into another reality.

You fell for the characters because they were not real.

You found people who wouldn't leave because they never existed.

With games, nobody knew who you were.

You played and became good because nobody knew you.

You weren't afraid to make friends because yet again, nobody saw you as the weird girl.

At the end of the day,the lessons taught you to stay humble.

Be grateful for what you have and become less materialistic.

Now you can view people from a different perspective.

You are overflowing with compassion and kindness.

The boundaries you built are strong and healthy.

Forgiving others easily because you understand their actions are a reflection of their internal struggles.

Thus, you understand nothing is personal.

It blessed you with the opportunity to heal before you start to truly live.

Relax with ease because you are no longer on survival mode.

Only people who love themselves are attracted to you.

Those people also inspire you to love yourself even more.

Finally, you accepted yourself for who you are.

Despite the world changing, you remained a lover girl.

It led you closer to God and drew you even closer to the spiritual path.
Stepping into your authentic self without the fear of other's opinions,
Has taught you to be confident in your own skin.

Coping Mechanisms

Human beings have a limit when it comes to feeling
pain.
We turn to coping mechanisms to ease off the pain.
Sometimes we turn to religion to create the illusion
that a higher being is taking away our pain.
You surrender to a higher being when the pain
consumes your body,
It becomes too much to bear.
Then you got the crystals where you imagine it sucking
in our pain away,
As a result, the crystals break when it consumes too
much negative energy.
Dancing is another way to shake off the torment,
Moving your body, swaying your hips from left to right,
Waving your arms in the air like you don't care,
Jumping while closing your eyes.

Feeling the grief flow away from your body and the happiness entering into it.

Coping mechanisms are temporary activities that release dopamine.

The more you heal, the more you begin to live with purpose.

The less distractions you have.

Power of Self Love

When you grow fond of anything, it sticks onto you.
When eating toffee, it sticks onto your teeth and it
stays there until you decide to remove it.
Now when you are a lover girl, you fall deeper.
The words cling onto you whenever a man tries to
pursue you.
Like a black hole, it exerts a strong gravitational force
that causes anything close enough to go inside.
That strong gravitational force represents our loving
energy.
Our heart widens its arms, ready to embrace our
partner's heart.
It opens our emotional cage, allowing us to become
vulnerable.
Loving thyself is not for the frail individuals.
Even though it aches when they don't love you the way
you deserve,
It gives you the power to walk away.

Choosing solitude should be a comforting choice.
After all, you are the only person you will spend most
of your life with.
Loving yourself makes letting go easier.
It will cause you to create firm boundaries for
self-respect.
Self-love will allow you to choose the ones who choose
themselves,
the same way you choose yourself.
If one isn't prioritizing themselves,
they won't be capable of cherishing you.
Choose those who choose themselves,
They will have an overflow of love to offer.

Detachment

Nothing belongs to us.

When we die, we go alone.

Our last thoughts are of ourselves.

It felt like God sat down with me and showed me my purpose,

Then I was fortunate enough to get a second chance to make it a reality.

In the process of my lessons, I learned nothing was mine.

No being, no pet, no career, no materials.

I was only responsible for the present tense.

It is impossible to control anything in life.

Holding on to the past means holding on to a reality that no longer exists.

Holding on to the future means holding on to a reality that doesn't exist yet.

Instead live in the present tense.

You have control over the little things you can do today to make a long term difference.

Be open minded and be open to changes.